BRITAIN IN OLD PHOTOGRAPHS

SEDGLEY & DISTRICT

A SECOND SELECTION

TREVOR GENGE

SUTTON PUBLISHING LIMITED

Sutton Publishing Limited
Phoenix Mill · Thrupp · Stroud
Gloucestershire · GL5 2BU

First published 1997

Cover photographs: *front*: Vale Cottage, Turls
Hill, Ettingshall village, *c*. 1900; *back*: the
Sedgley Village Brass and Reed Band, *c*. 1920.

British Library Cataloguing in Publication Data
A catalogue record for this book is available from the
British Library.

ISBN 0-7509-1486-6

Typeset in 10/12 Perpetua.
Typesetting and origination by
Sutton Publishing Limited.
Printed in Great Britain by
Ebenezer Baylis, Worcester.

A winter's scene showing 'the house on the rocks' in The Gorge, Hurst Hill, which was demolished in 1982.

CONTENTS

Introduction   5

1.   Streetscapes & Roads around the Manor   7

2.   Farms & Farming   21

3.   Houses Great & Small   31

4.   Churches & Chapels   49

5.   Shops & Services   65

6.   Public Houses   75

7.   The Industrial Past   83

8.   Schools   89

9.   Transport   95

10. A Miscellany of People, Life & Leisure   101

     Acknowledgements   126

The Beacon Monument, Sedgley.

The Beacon tower is certainly an icon for the area; both Sedgley and Coseley Urban District Councils included it in their coats of arms. As we see it today it is an 1846 rebuilding of an eighteenth-century monument tower, marking the spot of the historic beacon point. From its erection it appears to have been another important landmark of Sedgley. It actually stood just within the western border of the village of Ettingshall so both authorities could lay some claim to ownership. This John Price postcard (1904) shows it to have been one of those places that people walk to, particularly, in this case, for a breath of fresh air. Its splendid panoramas to the rolling countryside of the west, and the dense conurbation created by the Black Country to the east, make it still worth visiting. One of its local nicknames was 'the big whistle'.

INTRODUCTION

The name Sedgley has had two different interpretations. Firstly it described a single village with all of its associated lands to sustain that village's economy. Then it was the title of a much larger administrative area; an ancient manor and later a parish, formed from Sedgley and eight other villages. The 'mother' church stood in Sedgley village, where the present All Saints' stands. As today, its lofty steeple provided a landmark visible from far beyond the parish. Field paths and cart ways, whether for ecclesiastical or domestic and commercial reasons, all radiated from its axis, and travellers over the centuries have used it as the guide for their journey. It can be seen still, from as far as 20 miles away, when approaching from the west.

When local administration moved from the 'seat' of feudal government at the castle it was focused upon the parish. The parishes appeared to begin an administrative role from 1538 onwards, with increasing responsibility being added as the years progressed. Sedgley's parish records date from 1558 and are fortunately preserved. They reveal the names of the other eight villages for which the parish church cared and had jurisdiction over. Clearly the presence of no other church in the manor, and the building of a court house close to All Saints', ensured that the name of the village would remain the name of the manor, despite the growth of the other village communities. Yet these boundaries were still firmly in place at the Sedgley Tithe Survey of 1844, and because some of the boundaries were marked by natural features they still exist today. Even some of our man-made markers remain.

The reader may be surprised to find the locations and houses that some villages originally embraced. A map has been included within this second book, based upon the Tithe Survey, and showing the respective villages as they remained at that time. Included are several landmarks, mainly roads and churches; some were not present in 1844, but have been added for the benefit of the reader. If the map were superimposed upon a modern Ordnance Survey map all would be revealed!

Although two Anglican 'chapels of ease' had been built at Lower Gornal and Coseley before the Tithe Apportionment of 1844, in administrative terms it seems that the only concession had been to divide the parish by name into Upper and Lower Sedgley, appointing separate Board officers for the Poor, and so on.

The impact of non-conformity became increasingly significant from the seventeenth century onwards, but particularly in the nineteenth century, and here again loyalties would be formed which were not entirely hamlet- or village-based.

The eventual pressures of population and the inevitable granting of parish status for the chapels of ease would be the first obscurers of the old boundaries once beaten from Sedgley; a perambulation of 17½ miles. Yet it was not until the last decade of the nineteenth century that the Local Government Acts eventually saw the creation of Coseley as a self-governing unit for most of the eastern side of the old parish. In historical terms this independence could be described as short lived for the local government reforms that created the Metropolitan Boroughs of Dudley, Sandwell and Wolverhampton divided the entire area into three.

This second book also provides the opportunity of looking at some of the other villages of the manor in more detail than was possible in the first, particularly those of Coseley, Woodsetton, and Lower Gornal. Some of the forgotten boundary points are illustrated. Also, through the work of the photographers of the past, we can once more catch glimpses of a disappearing landscape and lifestyle. We can explore further that contradictory world, typical of the Black Country, of the numerous small farms of the area, that existed even within the industrial zones and, in some cases, were worked by the iron and coal masters themselves.

Most of the photographs are from the first half of this century, while some are from as recent a date as the 1960s and '70s. Some readers may find it difficult to think of these as 'old'. Some are there to show the remnants of available evidence of our past. That others record sites (and sights) already lost to us reveals how radical was the rebuilding and, in some cases at least, how careless of our heritage we were in those two decades!

STREETSCAPES & ROADS AROUND THE MANOR

Ark Terrace in Bourne Street stood well below road level, north of the Brook Inn; consequently it was in the village of Ettingshall. We see other old houses adjoined it and these were, in turn, against a property known as 'The Cuckoo's Nest'. In this photograph of March 1963 the terrace and houses are empty and awaiting demolition. Was the protective rail most necessary for customers leaving the inn?

View of Priory Lane, looking towards Vicar Street, 1975. In the centre of the picture the sunlight catches Gales Cottage (see page 35), and also the police station that stands on the site of the first Sedgley workhouse. The high wall to the right is of the old vicarage garden.

Moden Hill, nearing Ruiton, Upper Gornal, 1968. Modern buildings are just moving into a predominantly sandstone hamlet. There is strong evidence of the use of the local sandstone in the field and garden walls.

Fifty years ago a feature of the whole manor was the many single-storey cottages. This view of Spring (Vale) Road, Lanesfield, in Ettingshall village (previously Rookery Road at this point), illustrates some surviving in 1959.

Also dating from 1959, this picture of Ettingshall Road, approaching the Manor School, shows others. The shop in between has its walls waterproofed with 'gas'-tar. It also bears an enamel plate advert for Lyon's Tea. The durability of the advertising plates says much for product loyalties in those days. Many children going to school at The Manor will recall walking down the shop's steps, straight from the pavement into Mrs Hales' for their sweets.

The midday sunshine enhances this picture of houses on the east side of Brook Street, Woodsetton, 1959. They have that attractive look of houses built before the rigid road line was established, and therefore do not relate to it. They may have faced an older lane that twisted and turned, perhaps to ease the burden of horses carrying loads up the hill. The tree adds to the pastoral scene.

Looking north towards the same tree, the gable end of the house, left centre, shows it is much older than the others. It is built from the local stone and has a steeper roof line.

From the rear, the stone house reveals the tall chimney-stack of its brewhouse. Both house and brewhouse are recorded in the Tithe Schedule of 1844. The house would have been old even at that date, possibly one of the many that sprang up in the seventeenth century.

The photographer has shown that the stone house is backed by further brick houses. A woman peers interestedly through the sash window, and we glimpse a little part of one of those compact hamlet communities that grew up within our Manor. The houses were demolished in 1960.

Vale Street in the hamlet of Ruiton, Upper Gornal, 1970s. It shows that this one locality retained its stone buildings and walls longest.

Hill Street in Ruiton shows its stone qualities too as it climbs towards the brow, past the Durham Ox Inn, which is now a private house, and 'Dusty's' shop, now demolished. Beyond, the road drops steeply again to the old turnpike road to Dudley.

The view south, looking up Wolverhampton Road East towards Sedgley, in the Gibbons Hill area, reveals the breadth of the turnpike road at this point. Note the stone field walls on either side. Here, in 1968, it retains some of the lamp standards that had been tram poles and trolley bus wire carriers before supporting street lights.

Red Lane, Gospel End, is on the north side of Gospel End Road, and provides a contrast. It runs right to the Manorial boundary at Penn Brook. Its name is derived from the underlying clay that is only now seen beyond the tarmac access road to the Severn Trent Sewage Treatment Works built in 1963/4. This photograph was taken shortly after the road was made. In wet seasons the lane became almost impassable in parts.

Dudley Road, Upper Gornal, is again on the Dudley to Wolverhampton turnpike road, seen here in 1974. The terrace in the foreground, now demolished, shows prominent chimneys without pots, usually indicative of wood rather than coal burning. In Victorian times chimney pots became the essential requirement for burning coal without suffering from excess sulphur fumes indoors. Chimney pots were originally the privilege of the well to do. The further terrace and the stone field wall have survived.

These cottages, in old Gospel End village, stood on the south side immediately after passing through the sandstone cutting. An interesting feature was that electricity, for lighting, was brought into the house through conduits seen fastened to the exterior walls. The house next to the Rocks is featured on page 36. This photograph was taken in June 1975 not long before demolition.

Caddick Street, in The Coppice, Ettingshall village, 1951/2. Coppice Baptist Chapel, seen at the top of the picture, is featured on page 60. Demolition of the street began in the Autumn of 1960.

Parkes Lane, Woodsetton runs from Brook Street to Tipton Road, as seen here in 1959. Before the Tipton Road (turnpike) was cut in 1843 it ran right to Mons Hill, alongside the reservoir, to join the roads running from Wrens Nest and Upper Gornal. The houses pictured were demolished in the 1960s.

These houses on the eastern side of High Holborn, Sedgley, photographed in 1974, have survived, but not the stone wall. Neither has the advertisement on the gable end, already old at the time. It indicates a village of a size where a builder and carpenter can also make coffins, and provide a funeral service. Neither of his trades could occupy him fully! It would seem appropriate that a land parcel nearby bears the ancient name of Chit's Grave.

Bilston Street, Sedgley, 1971. This is the south side near to the High Street, The block to the left is older and bore the date-stone, inscribed 'BUILT 1845'. Mr E. Barwell lived in the end house and purchased the other three, renting them out and charging in 1940 8s or 8s 6d per week depending upon size.

Hollywell Street, Hurst Hill, Ettingshall, passes the old Waterhouse works, and the side of the sub-post office (both featured in Book 1) and reaches Hurst Hill. The shop facing Hollywell Street was a fish and chip shop owned by Laws.

Here the corner has been reached and we look up Hurst Hill, towards The Gorge. Next to the fish and chip shop (extreme right) is Mrs Williams, hairdresser. The Old Gate Hangs Well Inn can be seen nearer the top, while to its right a narrow passage led to the Old Row. Both photographs on this page are dated March 1962.

Bank Street, Coseley, July 1967. The small walled 'gardens' in front represent a step up the social ladder. A feature from around the last quarter of the nineteenth century onwards, it meant that the occupants were not faced with the prospect of stepping out directly on to the footpath, but had the benefit of a front garden. The lack of chimney pots is again evident. Bank Street was cut by the Birmingham New Road (1927) and a fragment of it remains on the opposite side of the road joining Mount Pleasant Street.

The junction of Legge Lane, Gough Road corner, Coseley, was a well built-up space in 1960. It now lies empty, aiding traffic visibility for modern transport needs.

New Street is in Lower Gornal village (though more usually referred to as Gornal Wood nowadays). In 1963 it was a mixture of Victorian dwellings occupying the sloping terrain of the village street.

Similarly Brook Street, Lower Gornal, slopes downwards with an even more diverse collection of housing styles. Those in the foreground show their workshops/brewhouses. Records and maps show that both were numerous.

Edge Street, Coseley village, in the area of Wallbrook, 1950s. This photograph conveys the compactness of the old community. Two chat at a doorway as a mother and child pause at a street shop. The public house, top right, is The Red Cow.

Wallbrook Street, Coseley, at its demolition in February 1959: a typical scene of the period. The old housing was in a poor condition and often insanitary, lacking the refinements that the post-war years required. Coseley's population was growing, and so the area was cleared. Some moved to new housing estates already built within the Urban District. The old housing gave way to new, in which three-storey flats figured greatly.

FARMS & FARMING

After the windmills came the steam mills. The remnants of this one near to Sedgley High Street can still be seen today from Bilston Street. The stone side of the old square mill has been used in the construction of this flat-topped building. There is a record of the mill being up for sale in 1833.

Lower Gospel End Farmhouse, Penn Road, 1976. The late Mr T.E. Pugh is on the right. It is much the same today and still has its stone barns. It is probably the oldest standing and habitable building in the Manor. It remains the home of the Pugh family, a family related to the Pughs featured in Book 1.

The date stone of the farmhouse. Its builder, or rebuilder, in 1695, records himself as H.B. It is thought that this may refer to a member of the Bourne family, later found in the Woodsetton area, and from whom Bourne Street gets its name.

Wood Farm, Cotwall End, is the site of a very ancient dwelling of Moysi le Forrester, and was once part of Himley Park. This photograph has been taken from the top of the old Baggeridge Colliery pit mound. In 1267 we learn that Moysi, son of Alan le Forrester, was pardoned for the death of one Stephen 'and any consequent outlawry'. Later, after the death of the Lord of the Manor in 1272, we learn that the rent of Moysi le Forrester was worth 'two pounds of pepper and two pounds of cumin'. Unusually, that rent was unchanged in an account for 1742.

A view across fields from Red Lane to the old barns of Gospel End Farm (shown in Book 1). The stone section of an older building has been incorporated into the new brick gable to add strength.

High Arcal Farm, Woodsetton, a beautiful view of this stone farmhouse that originated in the seventeenth century. In this 1950s photograph it is deserted, and demolition is inevitable. It had an unusual four-stack cruciform chimney at the centre.

Brownswall Farm, Gospel End Road, Gospel End. This drawing, by Ron Baker, shows the marked similarity of this stone farmhouse with that of High Arcal. Its fields provided the land for the late '50s housing estate that bears its name, though the farmhouse still stood in the early 1960s. Hamilton Close, a later development, now occupies most of the farmhouse site.

Fellows' Farm (some recall it as Fosters'), Woodsetton, a near neighbour to High Arcal Farm, 1960. The farm stood at the bottom of Rough Lane. Part of this lane survives, and is mostly used by the pupils of High Arcal School. Although now tarmacked, the footpath passes between the two hedgerows of the old lane as it leaves Tipton Road.

Fellows' Farm outbuildings were constructed from local stone, the dominant material until the second half of the nineteenth century. A walk to the farm down Rough Lane took you past a row of stone cottages on the left-hand side. The cottagers' water supply came entirely from a single spring.

Sandyfields Farmhouse in Cotwall End has survived, though in the photograph its gable window needed attention. It once lay on the old winding Sandyfield Road. The road has now been straightened at this point, leaving it the only building on this isolated stretch. It is stone built, but of the redder stone that is found nearby.

One of the brick-built barns has a dovecote incorporated in the gable. This use of roof space provided a valuable source of both fresh meat and eggs, particularly in wintertime, when only salted meat was available.

Ettingshall Park Farmhouse in 1956, shortly before demolition. Like many others, there has been a 'building on' of additional houses as owners wished to make their statement of personal wealth. An older house is seen to the left. The farm was once the home of the Feredays, Samuel II and his son Dudley, who were typical for their time – iron, coal masters and farmers. Local lore has it that, at their peak, they employed more people than any other man living! We do know that they were allowed to mint their own coins. The trees still grow on the housing estate that filled most of the farm fields.

A reminder of medieval farming are these ridges and furrows, still engraved in this field in Gospel End.

Hickmerelands Farm and barns, Sedgley, 1975. High mere is the origin of the name. This is another farm that became caught up in a modern housing development. In 1844 it was farmed by William Perry, though the lands then belonged to the Earl of Dudley. This century it is the Wooldridge family that most locals associate with Hickmerelands. The farm lies on a much-loved ancient footpath along King's Hill or 'Kinsell'. The farm has a wall with the date 1834, but it may well be older.

Springfield Farm, Sedgley. This photograph of about 1900 gives a rustic look to what appears to be a Georgian house. It lay close to the main Wolverhampton to Dudley road and has given its name to nearby Springfield Grove.

Woodcross Farm stood on the north side of Woodcross Lane, Ettingshall village, near to where the houses built for the police are today. This photograph of 1958 indicates its position in relation to the old houses across the lane. It had fragments of seventeenth-century construction, at least, and the high gable wall visible to the left of the chimney-stack might well indicate a thatched roof. Many people recall it as Head's Farm.

Two reminders of our past. On the left is an ancient stone stile post, leading from a footpath from Tenscore Field, Sedgley village. There would have been a matching one opposite. A stone slab would fill the slot and a branch or rod fit in as a top rail. On the right is an ancient oak roof timber, showing jointing slots and dowels, now serving as a kissing gate post in Gospel End village, near Red Lane Farm pictured in Book 1. Which building it originally came from is long forgotten, but perhaps the remnant of stone seen in Gospel End Farmhouse barn (page 23) could tell us?

J. C. BATES,

The Rookery Farm Dairy,

LANESFIELD,

Nr. WOLVERHAMPTON.

———

MILK SUPPLIED TWICE DAILY.

A dairyman's advertising card. In 1898 J.C. Bates, son of James Bates, bought Rookery Hall (see page 42). In 1899 he bought Rookery Farm. Dairying figured largely, as it did with most of the local farms, supplying the growing population. The farm stood on land occupied by the present Brynmawr Road.

Left: Today we forget the imperative need for all houses and farms to find and procure a water supply. An old pump in front of Lower Gospel End Farmhouse in 1976 is a reminder.

Right: Straits Farm, Cotwall End. This 'two-holer' toilet for adult and child was spotted at its demolition, *c.* 1976. It would have been an earth closet.

HOUSES GREAT & SMALL

The Gorge just west of the limestone ridge at Hurst Hill (see page 44).

Woodbank House, Cotwall End, stood almost at the bottom of the wide access road westwards from the first bend of Sandyfields Road. Just beyond the house the access narrowed into a field path. This photograph, taken in the 1950s, is of the front of the house. It was demolished at the end of the '50s.

This view of the house shows the attractive gardens and lawn. The two single-storey bays face due west and would have enjoyed magnificent views.

Another view of Woodbank House from the south shows how, like many others, it is the result of building on to a smaller house, seen on the right of the picture by the conservatory. The house had several occupants from Black Country industry including Ben Whitehouse, and also a Thompson. The elevated view is from trees that still stand behind Woodbank Road.

The Park Hall Hotel, Sedgley village, 1970s. The distinguished house at the centre was originally a home for the Lord of the Manor, and succeeded Willingsworth Hall in prominence when held by the Parkes family. The Ward family also lived here after the Manor was regained through marriage. The Wards moved to Himley in 1763, after being elevated to the Viscountcy of Dudley and Ward. Later the house became a Roman Catholic Seminary.

Parkes Hall, Woodsetton, 1835. One of the first water supply reservoirs of the area now covers the site. Significantly Parkes Hall pool is surrounded by a fine stone wall.

An old sketch of Willingsworth Hall, Brierley village. The hall has clearly been extended at different periods and shows some Tudor timbering. It became the home of the Parkes family after the purchase of the Manor. In the Hearth Tax of 1669/70 'Mrs Parkes de Willingsworth' was reported to have twenty-eight hearths, but boasted of forty. The assessor, commenting on the twenty-eight, says: 'but [she] refuseth to pay soe many'.

Gales Cottage, Sedgley village, 1975. Fortunately it still survives and provides a beautiful picture for people passing along Priory Lane. Continued family ownership is probably the reason it has remained largely unspoiled.

Bonnels, later Bonehill's Cottage, Ladymoor, Ettingshall – thought to have been the meeting place for the first Wesleyan Methodists in Ladymoor. The house garden was surrounded by a 'cinder wall', material readily available from nearby Capponfield Furnaces. It was photographed shortly before demolition in 1934. The old house bore a square stone plaque inscribed with 'FBE, 1726'. The letters stood for Frances Bonnel, Ettingshall.

Dormston House, Sedgley village, 1971, just before the furniture shop and offices were built on the garden land. Formerly called Sedgley Villa, it was owned by F.A. Homer (featured in Book 1). The last Homer to occupy the house was John Twigg Homer (see page 105), another prominent Sedgley resident who died in 1934. From that date the house lay empty until the Second World War when it was taken over by the War Office for Home Guard use. After the war it was purchased by J.R. Hickling, a local businessman and a local and county councillor.

Rock Cottage, Gospel End, 1974. This was the superior house at the end of the row shown on page 14, next to the sandstone cutting, hence its name. It was the home of the Austin family for many years.

Hill House, Upper Gornal, 1974. It was demolished in the 1980s. It was a substantial house of the area, and looks typically Victorian. The corner of the garden wall is protected by a cast-iron guard against carriage or cart wheels as entry is made to the rear for coach house and stabling.

A row on Bluebell Park, Woodsetton, photographed before the First World War. It shows how proudly the family posed outside this prestigious row, built by the Earl of Dudley for his limestone quarry managers and under-managers.

Mons Hill House, Woodsetton, was originally an engine house for the Earl's limestone quarries. The photograph, taken in about 1900, shows the Roberts family, father, mother, and daughter, who lived in this pleasant 'house conversion' for many years.

Preston's Row, Ladymoor, Ettingshall, 1960. The Swan Inn was at the far end of the row. In the distance, left, an arm of a beam engine can be seen and to the right two stacks of the steelworks.

Lanesfield Villa, Spring(vale) Road, Ettingshall, stood on the south side of the old Lanesfield Wesleyan Chapel (see page 59). Now divided into flats, it is remembered best as the home of the Johnson family, haulage contractors who began with horses and carts and progressed to lorries.

Vale Cottage, Turls Hill, Ettingshall village, *c*. 1900. It is believed that this photograph shows members of the Fullwood family. The brook that runs a little to the rear of the cottage is the boundary between Woodsetton and Ettingshall. In 1877 Isaac Fullwood worked for the Whitehouse family, a well-known local iron and coalmaster. Ben Whitehouse, a son of the founder, lived in the grand Turls Hill House further up the lane. Ben's son Henry writes in his diary of accompanying Isaac Fullwood on their walk to work at the Priorfields Ironworks at Deepfields.

On their journey they would have passed this property, also in Turls Hill Road and seen here at its demolition. The leaning wooden prop partly hides the fact that there was once a beer seller here. The picture below shows the gable end on the left as once being part of an extensively timber-framed structure.

Rookery Hall, Lanesfield, Ettingshall, 1980s. It was purchased in 1898 by James Charles Bates, son of James Bates, the founder, in 1840, of the brickworks in Spring Road, which continued until 1956. It is now The 44 Club, established after the Second World War by those formerly active in Civil Defence. It stands on what is a very ancient house site. A map of 1834 shows it as Lane's Hall. The Lanes were a well-known and influential family originating at Bentley Hall. In 1844 it is shown as Ettingshall Hall, probably an older title. The sub-letting of Ettingshall just after 'Domesday' in 1088 suggests that this might even be the site of the dwelling of the landowner.

This little cottage stood at the entrance gate to Rookery Hall, photographed just after 1900. It was known as Grainger's Cottage as Mrs Grainger lived in it; she worked at the hall.

Hollydene, Coseley village. J.C. Bates built this house for the benefit of local Liberals. Its opening ceremony was performed by Prime Minister William Gladstone; Mrs Gladstone was also present and received a bouquet. The Liberal party were unable to meet their financial responsibilities and J.C. Bates re-possessed the house for his own use, and lived there until purchasing Rookery Hall. It still stands in the isolated corner of Hayward Street, off Mount Pleasant Street.

Ettingshall House, Highfields Road (formerly Capponfield Road), c. 1958. Here again, as with Bonnels on page 35, there seems to be no doubt about which village this house is situated in. Although of indeterminate age, its Georgian-style frontage and double-stack appearance suggest a modified older building.

The Gorge, Hurst Hill, Ettingshall. This is one of the homes that has a connection with the Whitehouse family. It is built right on the limestone, and the house was shielded from the smoky east by the ridge itself. Here two Whitehouses, with dog, pose for the photograph. The house still exists but was privately purchased in the 1950s or '60s. Unfortunately its pitched roof was removed and replaced by a low single-pitched one. It is currently in the possession of Wolverhampton Metropolitan Borough, and is used for educational purposes.

Woodthorne, the impressive home of the Marsh family (see page 119) in Lower Gornal. It was at Cooper's Bank, Himley Road. Known locally as The Mansion, it was demolished when Grosvenor Road was developed, and today Woodthorne Close stands upon the site.

This little cottage stood in Brook Street, Woodsetton, and is seen here in October 1959. Originally built of stone, it had been heightened, by brick courses and dormer windows, to create a second storey. This alteration itself was made some time before the photograph was taken. The dormer windows and also that in the gable are typically of Victorian cast iron, no doubt locally made, and much favoured at the time.

The Mount in Fereday's Croft, Sedgley, from the field path south of Bush Bank, or Behind Cox's. The stone field wall has been maintained, but the croft is now filled with modern housing. The house, with its walled garden intruding into the croft, is one of the several 'Mounts' to be found in this hilly area. It was demolished to make way for a small development of executive homes.

This house, photographed in the 1960s, still stands in the Coppice, Woodsetton. It has had many owners, including Chesterman's the bakers, who also had a single-storey shop adjoining. Previously Charles Beach, who had a butcher's shop in Horace Street, lived there. Older residents recall a corn barn standing nearby.

This 'country' cottage in Havacre Lane, Deepfields, Coseley, has had to protect itself from the results of local mining. The external tie bars that surround it in this photograph of 1974 are typical of so many Black Country buildings.

Woodsetton House, home of the Goughs, was photographed in 1955 when it was already empty and awaiting demolition. The Mormon church now occupies the site.

Railway Terrace, Coseley, stood (with this wing facing into the Stour Valley Line Cutting) quite near to Coseley Hall. Here it is in May 1967 shortly before demolition.

A row of terrace houses in Bilston Street, Sedgley, had a stone at their centre inscribed Goodfellows' Terrace. Photographed in 1971, the houses were demolished just a few years later.

No. 1 Vale Street, Ruiton, was a typical Gornal stone house in the old hamlet. Photographed in the 1970s, it has now been demolished.

CHURCHES & CHAPELS

A relic of the Manor's religious, industrial past: ironmaster John Wilkinson's pulpit, made from cast iron for what was known locally as the Cast Metal Meeting House. The chapel has long gone but the pulpit is still used by Bradley Methodists.

All Saints' Church Choir, Sedgley, 1953. Back row, left to right: J. Evans, H. Avery, C. Pennel, T. Wright, G. Porter, W. Cox, M. Wilson, K. Slater, J. Hancock, A. Hughes (hidden), J. Sneyd, H. Bullock, A Malpass, W. Rushton, H. Lloyd, Mr Perks. Middle row: T. Hartland, R. Lavender, D. Price, L. Billingham (organist), Revd Wm Sargeant (vicar), Revd B. Skelding (curate), R. Shinton (choirmaster), ? Jones, ? Timmins, ? Smith, G. Sneyd. Front row: A. Billingham, ? Friend, ? Malpass, ? Benton.

In the spring of 1975 All Saints' Church had its bells recast. This one, seen in the porch, was the 'passing' bell and the largest of the peal. It was removed with more difficulty than the rest for it was one of those that had been present in the old tower when the new tower had been built around it in 1829. It bore the chilling Latin inscription 'Hodie mihi, cras tibi, 1720' – 'Today for me, tomorrow for thee'.

Homer's Chapel, Sedgley. When the church was rebuilt the demolition of the old church resulted in the exposure to the atmosphere of what had been the Homer Chapel. The vaults are seen clearly in this photograph of 1972. One of the family buried here was F.A. Homer, featured in Book 1. A further loss to the chapel was the removal of the iron railings that surrounded each vault. This was during a metal collection, to aid the war effort, in the 1940s.

After churchyard space became short a new burial ground was given by the Earl of Dudley in 1808. He also gave land to provide a road access to the main entrance in Vicar Street. This linked Dudley Street to Bush Bank. Later another graveyard was opened, with more workable soil, north of Gospel End Street. Many will remember this graveyard as pictured, overgrown and neglected, until it was landscaped by the local authority. It had seen some notable interments, among them Dr Isaiah James Baker, beloved doctor of Hurst Hill, and Joseph Nicholds, musician and composer whose most famous work, the oratorio *Babylon*, is still occasionally performed locally.

Sedgley parish church children gather behind the National School dressed up in costume for an occasion. It may be a Queen's ceremony, or a May Festival; certainly there is a look of St George's Day costume about many of the children.

The Parish Vestry that once stood at the top of Dean Street. Here, parish business was conducted and the Boards of Health were formed that dealt with the cholera outbreaks of 1832 and 1849. It became redundant when the new Parish Hall was built in the vicarage grounds.

Though retouched, this picture postcard of Christ Church, Coseley, in about 1905, enables us to view the building without the trees that now surround it. It was built as a chapel of ease for Lower Sedgley and opened in 1830, one year after the rebuilding of the parish church. It was to be the means whereby the old parish could be divided into two.

Ettingshall parish church, Millfields Road, 1956. It was the cholera epidemic of 1832 that was to result in this church being built. When the vicar of Sedgley recognized how great was the population at the north end of the parish, and also the impact of Ettingshall New Village that was being built outside the parish north of Millfields Road, he determined to put a church at the edge of his parish near to the turnpike gate at Catchems Corner. The foundation stone was laid in May 1834 and in 1835 the church opened.

Time alters circumstances and Ettingshall parish church was eventually to be resited on Ettingshall Park, close to The Beacon. It was dedicated in 1961. This was to meet the needs of the new area being created by Ettingshall Park Farm estate. It resulted in the old church being demolished soon after this date.

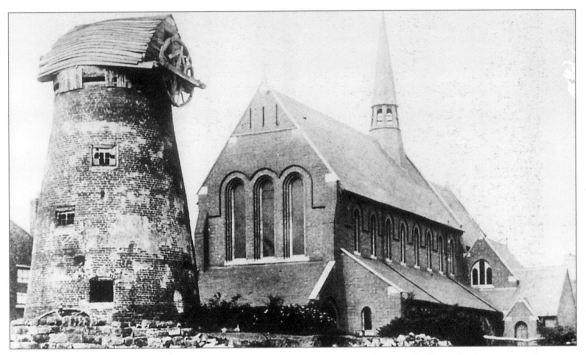

St Chad's Church, Coseley, makes an interesting picture with Coseley Windmill in the foreground. It became the centre of the new parish of West Coseley at its opening in 1884. As was usually the case with Anglican expansion in the Manor, the Earl of Dudley both gave the land and provided a significant donation. The church appears to be very new and probably dates the photograph for us; the state of the windmill at that time can also be seen.

The Chapel House, Club Row, Upper Gornal. Non-conformity often began in a house meeting, and Chapel House got its name first from housing the Wesleyan Methodists until they opened their chapel in Kent Street in 1832. Later, when the Methodist New Connexion movement was gathering strength locally, they followed the Wesleyans by using Chapel House until their own chapel, Mount Zion, was completed in 1878. (Both churches feature in Book 1)

The mission church of St Barnabas in Gospel End. This little church on Wodehouse Road and Penn Road was another church that was built during the Anglican expansion of the late nineteenth century. It has now been converted into a private residence.

The Unitarian Church, Avenue Road, Coseley. The foundation of the original church goes back to 1662 when the vicar of Sedgley was the Revd Joseph Eccleshall. Failing to sign the Act of Uniformity, he was ejected from his living and eventually established an Independent, or Presbyterian congregation in a house at Old End, Coseley. The first church that followed was affected by mining subsidence, and this building was opened in August 1875.

The entrance to Ruiton United Reform Church, Upper Gornal. This church might trace its origins to the ejection of Sedgley's vicar. An independent cause seems to have been established in the area from around the middle of the eighteenth century, greatly influenced by the Underhill family. Several of the Underhill family had served as churchwardens; John Underhill, a descendant, being inspired by the preaching of the Revd George Whitfield, formed a group that resulted in a chapel being erected in 1777. Enlarged in 1804, this still proved inadequate. In 1830 the present chapel was completed.

Ruiton Chapel, Hermit Street, Lower Gornal (previous page) is in the Classical style (as were many non-conformist buildings of this period), and built from the local stone. It appears in the RCHME book of non-conformist chapels of Shropshire and Staffordshire.

Darkhouse Baptist Sunday school, Darkhouse Lane, Coseley. It stood on the opposite side of Darkhouse Lane to the church. Built in 1833, it was photographed here in 1966. It was demolished a few years later when new school premises were opened at the side of the church building.

Hurst Hill Wesleyan Church, Ettingshall. The original church (1798) stood on the opposite side of the road, then known as Can Lane. This church, in the classical style, is of 1864. The photograph, from around the turn of the century, shows in the foreground Kossuth (Kosser) Fellows, William and Albert Screen and George Cooper. The church no longer has its gate pillar lights, and the gable has been rebricked – losing the dated inscription that read 'Wesleyan Methodist MDCCCLXVII'.

Lanesfield Wesleyan Chapel, Spring Vale Road, Ettingshall (also featured in Book 1), photographed in 1934; there had been a church on this site since 1834. The clock tower has been removed, because of the fear of subsidence, and the new schoolroom had been added to the right in 1909.

Coppice Baptist Chapel, Ettingshall, is the oldest standing religious building in the Manor that has not undergone change. The church building remains much as it has always been since its building in 1804. The large additional building at the rear dates from 1875. Its one concession to age and site are the reinforcing plates 'tying' the building.

Cinderhill Primitive Methodist Chapel dates from 1850. Photographed here in 1960, it shows some of the houses of its old community still around it. The high steps to the front door of the house to the right show how the builder had to deal with the steeply sloping land. At the rear there is a glimpse of Johnson Street.

Roseville Wesleyan Chapel, The Square, Coseley, 1960. This was the second chapel; opened in 1853, it succeeded another earlier chapel described as being 'in Mamble Square, near Summerhouse Row and subject to subsidence'. A third church has now been built near the new Coseley by-pass.

Zoar New Connexion Methodist Church, Lower Gornal. This is a surprising picture for those knowing today's church. It was taken for the Jubilee celebrations in 1904. The fifty-year anniversary was the spur for the rebuilding that resulted in the present church. This photograph provides a pleasing record of a long-forgotten building.

Sedgley Wesleyan Chapel, Bilston Street, was opened in 1849. The Wesleyans moved to the High Street in 1904 (see Book 1). The little chapel was at one time known as Lane's Chapel, because of the strong influence of the Lane family. Among their ancestors was Jane Lane, who rode from Bentley Hall with her future monarch (Charles II) disguised as her groom, effecting his escape to the Continent. This photograph, taken in 1969, shows it in its original form before its re-orientation and refurbishment by the Sedgley Full Gospel Church, its most recent congregation.

One of the features of the Methodist cause in the High Street during the 1960s was its weekly coach service to the new housing estates of Brownswall Farm, Sedgley Hall and Northway, to collect children for Sunday School.

The Methodist Chapel at Wallbrook, Coseley, was erected in 1839. It was also often known as Ebenezer, a name normally associated with a Coseley Baptist Church, shown in Book 1. It was photographed here in 1956, shortly before its demolition, in company with many of the old streets of Wallbrook, shown on page 20. Like its streets, Wallbrook Methodist Church was rebuilt.

Another Chapel House, this one in Roberts Street, Lower Gornal. So many non-conformist causes started with such a building. This one has survived as a private house.

Mount Zion Methodist, Upper Gornal. Shown here is the Sunday School Anniversary 'Platform'. The choirmaster (left) is Mr John (Jack) Amphlett and the organist (right) is Mr John Grainger.

SHOPS & SERVICES

Many little shops disappeared with the housing in the 1970s. This little tobacconist was at 14 Abbey Street.

The older shops in Dudley Street, Sedgley, got new façades at street level. This photograph from 1972 shows an old carriage entrance preserved, and some old shop windows surviving. The Concord Centre has not yet been built, though the footings seen in the garden of Dormston House (page 36) have grown into the new shop and office block.

One fondly remembered shop, next to the Sedgley Pound (or Pinfold) was The Original Tobacco Shop. Older residents remember being sent as children by parents and grandparents to get pipe tobacco cut from the 'twist'.

J.T. Egginton's began life as a prominent store in Sedgley Bull Ring. It was well featured in Book 1 as Sedgley General Store and Sedgley Drug Store; because of its pharmacy, Mr Egginton became one of Sedgley's first photographic recorders. This is a less familiar view of the shop taken from Dudley Street, and again by the owner.

This picture was taken by a more recent photographer in the 1970s, before the building's demolition. It shows the Victorian Gothic style of the architecture, even down to the decorative stonework. The author was once permitted to take photographs of the Bull Ring from these upper windows, and noticed that the main roof beam bore the motto 'Long Live the Proprietor' in large white letters.

Dudley Street, Sedgley. Traffic approaching the Bull Ring in the early 1970s is still a well-remembered scene for most local residents. The ground-floor room, seen here as a hairdressers, right of picture, had once been the tram waiting room.

This view in the opposite direction, towards the Grand Junction Inn, is an elevated view of the scene at the top of page 66. It was taken from Egginton's fire escape (previous page). The trees at top left are those remaining in the garden of Dormston House.

Two John Price postcards capture the atmosphere of The Square, Roseville, Coseley, early this century. The first shows the block containing the post office. Tunnel Street runs left, named in recognition of the canal tunnel (see page 100) that lies well beneath it, towards Fullwood's End. To the right of the post office is Avenue Road.

This view of The Square catches the coach entrance on the left and makes Roseville Wesleyan Chapel (page 61) its focal point. The trees concealed Roseville House, another large residence with impressive grounds. It was once the home of W.H. Hawthorne, a director of Cannon Industries, who obviously believed in living near the job.

Coseley had an earlier post office than the one shown on the previous page. It was The Bazaar, a popular emporium. The proprietors, Mr and Mrs Mills, stand outside the shop with their assistants early this century. Next door was George Mason's grocers, on Bank Street corner.

A view of The Square from Castle Street corner, *c.* 1965. It shows the post office, but reveals that The Bazaar is now the home of Clarke's Radio.

Percy Richardson's chemist shop, in Lower Gornal, was a local institution from the 1930s to beyond the end of the Second World War. Even here, converted partly to a cobbler's shop, the name is maintained above the door. It stood on the corner of Brook Street and Abbey Street.

The right-hand house is 15 Abbey Street, Lower Gornal. For the last years of its life it reverted to a private dwelling, but it had first been a corn shop, and from 1905 until 1968 traded as Jones's newsagents and tobacconists, until the business transferred to Abbey Road. In the '60s twenty-two paper boys delivered 2,000 evening newspapers from the old shop. It also acted as delivery point for Sunday newspapers for a much wider area, stretching as far as Pensnett. The papers were stored and sorted in the entry. The building was demolished in 1977.

New Street, Lower Gornal, and Elizabeth Hair Fashions occupies a double-fronted shop.

This single-storey shop was a doctor's surgery between the '30s and '40s, and later it became a ladies' hairdressers. Here it is seen as a gents' hairdressers in the 1970s. Red Hall School can be seen over the wall to the right.

Woodward's the pawn brokers, Gospel End Street, Sedgley, early this century. It has now become part of the premises of Aspect Lighting. Mrs Mary Catherine Woodward ran the shop, and in 1924 she could advertise 'established for over half a century'.

Here in Brook Street and Bird Street, Lower Gornal, is an example of that vanishing feature of Victorian streets: a corner shop that has a 'neutral' and welcoming entrance to both streets. Overtaken by the supermarket era, it is now a private residence.

Dusty's, Hill Street, Ruiton, Upper Gornal. This stone-built house and shop (that had been added later) were demolished, quite recently – the last stone shop in Ruiton.

Left: The Bakery in Prospect Row, Lower Gornal – remembered as Griffiths's and then Round's. We forget the local breadmaking that was once a feature of each village's life.
Right: Sedgley Gas Works was in Lower Gornal. It sometimes served its community like a shop. When pressure was being reduced through use by Gibbon's Works furnaces, the workmen would climb up and put weights on the top of the gas holder to help Gornal dinners to be cooked in time.

SECTION SIX

PUBLIC HOUSES

The Ivy House, Coseley. A fairly recent casualty, it was demolished in about 1992. Its old function changed in 1985 when it first closed. It opened in 1987 as an Italian restaurant, but later reverted to a public house. After the pub's demolition the land served as a car sales area, and now provides the Birmingham New Road with a drive-in burger restaurant.

The Hop and Barley Corn, Mason Street, Coseley, photographed just prior to its demolition in about 1957. Its most famous landlord proved to be Joseph Nicholds, an extraordinary local musician, who first worked for Wombwell's Menagerie Band, and rose to writing religious songs and cantatas (see page 51). The new Hop and Barleycorn was built at the side on the same plot. 'As one door shut, another opened?'

The Ship and Rainbow Inn, Rainbow Street, Coseley, 1957. Many of our local streets bore no official name until the 1880s, when rate collecting became difficult owing to the duplication of local names. The inn obviously predates this road's designation. As the old houses were demolished and rebuilt, so was the Ship and Rainbow

The Golden Lion, Ash Street, Daisy Bank, Brierley village, 1960. This is another public house that has now been rebuilt to keep up with the times.

The Summer House Inn, Swan village, Woodsetton, 1960. The confusion of doors suggests that more than one cottage was used to create this inn. There were at least three Summer House Inns in the Manor. One is in Gospel End village, another in School Street, Coseley, and this one, which still stands in Woodsetton.

The Druid's Head in Caddick Street, the Coppice, Ettingshall. Each hamlet within the village seemed to be well served by more than one house. The Coppice area could support quite a few, but the Druid's Head seemed particularly popular. It went with the Coppice demolition in 1960. Joe Adams is recalled as the landlord before Joseph Flavell.

The Black Horse, Upper Ettingshall Road, Ettingshall. Most people are aware of the White Horse in Upper Ettingshall Road, at its junction with Hurst Hill. A few doors up is a general stores and, in this photograph of 1960, it seems to be concentrating on selling newspapers. The shop is still there today and few remember it as the Black Horse.

The Talbot, Cinderhill, Ettingshall, 1957 – when it already seems to be delicensed. It was an unusual inn in having no Sunday licence. Some will remember it as the site of a changing room for footballers about to play on the pitch near to Monument Lane, with the precarious slopes of The Beacon to add interest to the game.

The Apple Tree stood on a corner in Castle Street, Coseley. It is seen here in the June sunshine of 1960. When Wallbrook was redeveloped a new Apple Tree was built in Central Drive, near to Old End Lane; from the new position it could serve both its existing and a new clientele.

The Anchor Inn, Deepfields, Coseley, 1957. A whole community existed alongside the canal, as the adjoining houses show. Now only Anchor canal bridge remains. The field next to the Anchor was the site for Lower Sedgley's celebration of The Annual Wake. Stories are told of riders in the swing boats squealing with delight as they rode out over the canal and saw the water beneath.

The Beacon Hotel, Bilston Street, Sedgley. It is still a popular house, famous for its home-brewed ale, and still in the hands of the Hughes family.

The Brook Inn, Brook Street, Woodsetton is little changed today since this photograph of 1974. It is only just in Woodsetton in an important position; the early deeds show that the landlord was required to maintain the bridge over the brook that flows to the right (north) of the pub. Left (or south) of the brook is Woodsetton; north of the brook is Ettingshall; while on the opposite side of the road lies the village of Coseley. The inn was an important landmark.

The Union Mill, 'Catchems' Corner', Ettingshall, is seen here framed by the railway bridge that provided part of the platform for the elevated Ettingshall Road railway station (LNWR). Now demolished, the Union Mill stood close to the Manor boundary, which runs along the middle of the road here.

The Horse and Jockey, Hall Lane, Cinderhill, lies within another of those old centres of community that grew up without a road to relate to. The oldest building on the right is the old Horse and Jockey, which closed when the new one was built nearby across Hall Lane.

Job Horton's builder's yard and DIY store, Tipton Street, Sedgley, has been established for many years. The Dormston Garage, seen here underneath in the 1960s, may even have been forgotten. Few know of its earlier function, for it was built by Thomas Barr in 1848 as a malt house, and he pursued his trade here for twenty years.

THE INDUSTRIAL PAST

Thomas Perry Ltd, Highfields Works, stood on the Brierley side of the road that divided Brierley from Ettingshall. This photograph, from 1960, is of an old-established company. The Beacon tower was rebuilt in honour of Thomas Perry in 1846 by his friend Lord Wrottesley. The buildings stand, but under new management.

The Cannon Iron Foundry, Coseley, from where Whitehouse's Iron Works once stood, 1964. The Birmingham Canal Navigation runs between the two sites, serving both, and made the delivery of iron and shipping of finished products very easy.

The heavy reliance of local industry upon manpower, together with pride in the job, seem to be the two features revealed by this Cannon photograph from before the First World War.

The Cannon possessed a James Watt engine, seen here with its two proud operators, D. Peplow (left) and E. Crispin (right).

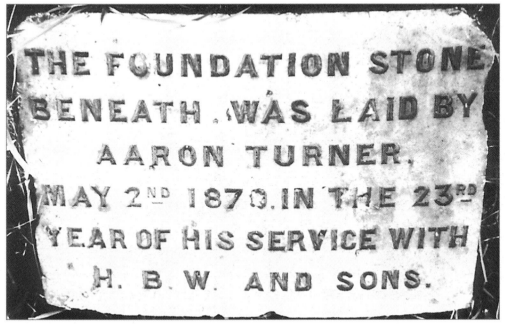

A Whitehouse's furnaces relic from Deepfields, Coseley. This ceramic block, found at Hurst Hill in 1937, reminds us of the management's desire to honour faithful service. H.B.W. stands for the founder, Henry Bickerton Whitehouse. The same initials are carved on the right of All Saints' porch, Sedgley, as a reminder that the Whitehouse memorials are within.

The works of W. & S.S. Allen, Upper Ettingshall Road, 1967, shortly before demolition. They were the makers of screws, nuts and bolts, and provided 'outwork' for some local people. Modern housing now occupies the site.

A brick kiln at William R. Mobberley's Victoria Firebrick Works, Upper Ettingshall Road, Breen Ridding, March 1964.

Ben Parkes, Woodsetton Works, Brook Street, 1960. Established early in the nineteenth century, they were the makers of small ironware of any pattern, and specialized in fenders and fire irons. Modern housing has replaced this old-established firm, which was on the west side of Brook Street.

A winding house for cables from the limestone workings on Wrens Nest, Woodsetton. It is seen here in a ruinous state in the late 1950s.

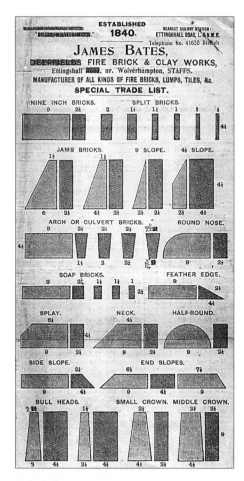

James Bates, firebrick patterns, Spring (Vale) Road, Ettingshall. The works traded from 1840 to 1956. At the time of its foundation, by James Bates of Old End House, the brickworks would have been part of Manor Road. Where there were collieries there were often brickworks using the clay adjacent to the coal. Many small brickworks would have existed, particularly in Lower Sedgley. When Baggeridge Pit opened in Gospel End this century (see Book 1), it was not long before an adjacent brickworks was opened. It has survived beyond the life of that colliery.

James C. Bates, having bought Rookery Farm, could not resist seeking the treasure that lay beneath. A colliery was opened in one of his fields, and here he poses with pipe outside the 'hovel' that he has constructed, without foundations, for his colliers to take their meals in, early this century.

SECTION EIGHT

SCHOOLS

The playground of the Sedgley National Schools, opened in 1828 (featured in Book 1).

SEDGLEY
INFANT SCHOOL.

CHILDREN from Four to Six Years old will be admitted into this School on **MONDAY, JULY 5,** at 9 o'Clock.

Children from Two to Four Years old will be admitted at the same Hour on the **MONDAY** following.

Payment of each Child Two-pence weekly; to be paid every Monday Morning in advance.

T. Simpson, Printer, Wolverhampton.

Advertising the presence of the school may have been an old form of junk mail. It provides the reminder to us that education was not free until the end of the nineteenth century, nor were the sums requested as paltry as they now seem. There are records also of a 'three for the price of two' sales incentive!

Miss Smith agrees with the Rev'd C. Girdlestone to be mistress of the Infant School and superintend the girls Sunday School, Sedgley, and to receive for salary two pence a week from each child, and £5 a quarter from the treasurer of the schools; payable March 25, June 24, September 29, December 25; and the use of the house adjoining the schools. Each party to be entitled to one quarter of a year's notice from either of the above days.

C Girdlestone
August 22. 1835.   Louisa Smith

An original contract from the National School provides a fascinating insight into the role and the payment of teachers. The signature is of Sedgley's most famous and influential vicar (he got quite a write-up in the *Dictionary of National Biography*). As Charles Girdlestone retired in 1837 to be succeeded by William Lewis, his curate, the date must be interpreted as 1835.

Tudor School, Clarence Street, Upper Gornal, recently demolished, was one of the remaining board schools of the Manor. The term board school has been retained in the housing that now occupies the site.

Daisy Bank Board School survives in old Brierley, though now as a community centre and not as a school.

Two views of Mount Pleasant Primary School, Ivy House Lane, Coseley. It was demolished in about 1990 and replaced by new housing. One headmaster, much remembered by the older residents, was Stan Grange. On the same campus, the old senior school has survived and now serves as the Local History and Archives centre for the Metropolitan Borough of Dudley. This became superfluous as a school when Coseley High School, off the eastern limb of Ivy House Lane, opened in 1969. Another well-remembered headmaster at the senior school was Richard Earp, writer of a play for the school's children called *A Country called Black*. It aimed to create local pride in the area's past.

Coseley Old Meeting School, glimpsed through the garden of Railway Terrace, 1965. Listed as an endowed charity of the Presbyterian Meeting House in 1790, it ceased being a day school at Easter 1881. In 1890 the Charity Commissioners allowed the Trustees to allocate the endowment 'in the Advancement of the Education of children who are *bona-fide* Residents of the Parish of Sedgley'.

Queen Victoria School, Bilston Street, Sedgley. The photograph shows the children in Standard 1 photographed in the year of 1934. Back row, left to right: Harry Challenger, Billy Wilkins (or Watkins?), George Aston, -?-, Ray Wilson, Les Bevan, Cliff Bennett, Reg Upton, Harold Bradley, Reg Price. Fourth row: George Cox, Reg Clark, Tom Morgan, Gordon Stanley, Jo Elwell, Herbert Bond, Jack Williams, Joseph Johnson, Cyril Giles, Harry Jeavons, Mr Eddinsberry. Third row: -?-, Doug Fellows, Tom Shaw, Reg Guest, Reg Jones, Allan Dransfield, John Smith, Reg Wildblood, Jimmy Overton, Benny Meese. Second row: Aubrey Pace, Joe Simner, -?-, Joe Morgan?, Hayward Bennett, Tom Harris, Harold Jones, Ben Hickman?. Front row: Henry Smith, -?-, Andrew Harper, Fred Hartill, Arthur Webb, Billy Webb, Harold Wilkes, Harold Nicholls. Two who are well known in the district today are Fred Hartill, who grew up to be a local butcher, but internationally famous for owning the champion show jumper *Pennwood Forge Mill*, and George Cox, life-long champion of Scouting in Sedgley. Queen Victoria School was built in 1897 and therefore is now past its centenary. It was built in that great flourish of national and royal pride that emanated from the Diamond Jubilee.

TRANSPORT

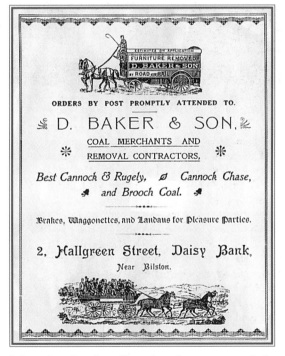

This 1911 advert for D. Baker & Son, Brierley village, shows how important the horse once was and also the need to be versatile. Principally a coalman, Mr Baker would also provide transport for pleasure parties — one would hope not in the same vehicles!

Askew Bridge Toll House stands in Lower Gornal, literally at the junction with Cotwall End village and Himley. It is the only remaining tollhouse still in its place in the Manor. It has been used as a private dwelling since the decommissioning of the Turnpike Trust, but quite recently it has been extended at the rear, though without any detraction from this appearance. It was also known locally as the 'Pop House' because of the home-made pop sold from there.

After the tram, the trolley bus. This single decker passes through Sedgley Bull Ring in the 1920s, heading for Wolverhampton on a rainy day. Although much missed, people still smile at the losing of connection as the poles slipped from the overhead wires, and at the conductor's attempts to put them back.

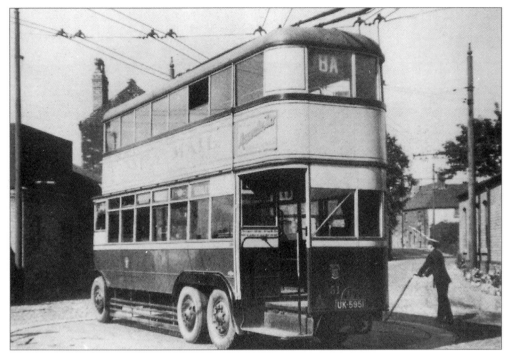

In contrast to the previous picture, this double-decker trolley bus gets turned on the turntable that stood in front of the old depot off Valley Road, Upper Gornal. The warmth of the sun can almost be felt.

As well as tradespeople, people of means kept horses well after the invention of the motor car. Doctors often rode on them, industrialists still kept their carriages, and even mine host from the local pub would enjoy his rides out in a horse and trap. This is Robert (Bob) Bates, youngest son of J.C. Bates at Rookery Hall, in about 1920.

This carriage belonged to W.H. Hawthorn, Cannon Foundry director, who lived at Roseville House, as recorded on page 69. The liveried coachman is Mr William West, of Castle Street, Coseley.

The Pound, Dudley Street, Sedgley village, survived and was very occasionally used just into the 1970s. Today the position of All Saints' and the pedestrian crossing mark exactly where it was.

The charabanc was destined to take over from D. Baker's brakes and waggonettes. Here in the 1920s these happy 'trippers' have dressed up for a day out. Notice the solid tyres, the carbide headlights and the warning horn positioned outside and blown by the driver, who leaned out and squeezed the rubber air ball.

Cap at a jaunty angle, posing in front of his charabanc, this driver waits before taking what looks to be a ladies' outing. He may be going no further than Kinver, but one can be sure the journey itself will be an adventure.

The earliest planned transport is represented by Coseley canal tunnel, which is 360 yards long (328 m). It was pivotal to the successful completion of Thomas Telford's new main line from Birmingham to Wolverhampton, which eliminated the most tortuous section of the James Brindley canal of 1770. The tunnel was opened on 6 November 1837, unusually having a tow path on either side. The road restraining wall, here shored up against the significant crack, is to the northern side of Ivy House Lane. This John Price postcard rather exaggerated the length of the tunnel to ¾ mile.

A steam locomotive pulls a passenger train towards Deepfields on the Up line to London, past Stewart & Lloyds Bilston steelworks and with an empty canal as its companion. Here in 1951 we look at a world that has already changed dramatically and will continue changing.

A MISCELLANY OF PEOPLE, LIFE & LEISURE

A family in the 1920s sit in the Pleasure Grounds at Dudley Castle, Woodsetton village, before the zoo has been thought of. The grounds were opened on special days, bank holidays and so on, and drew crowds from as far as Birmingham.

This beautiful picture is of Clara Bates (née Meeson) in the grounds of Rookery Hall, *c.* 1900. Having left Brewood with her family to emigrate to America, she left the ship on seeing her husband to be on Liverpool Quayside. He had come to wave her off! They married at Christ Church, Coseley, in 1874.

Ben Whitehouse's Turls Hill House has often been referred to as 'The Belgians'. The Whitehouses' business failed before the First World War and as the house was empty it was commandeered by the War Office to house Belgian refugees. Here, in about 1916, a group of them gather on the lawn of what appears still to be a very fine house.

A group of customers outside the Five Ways Inn, Himley Road, Lower Gornal, before the First World War. They are, left to right, 'Happy' Tom Hickman, Walter Gutteridge, Billy Marsh, Mark Hicken, Billy Fellows and Freddy Worton. Walter Gutteridge was killed in the First World War and Mark Hicken died in a pit. Billy Marsh was the publican's son, and he is the one to possess a carbide lamp on his bicycle!

It could be a country scene, but it is in Lanesfield, Ettingshall, surrounded by pits and lime works. The horses seem an integral part of the family.

Left: May Richards (née Bates), the little girl who presented Mrs Gladstone with her flowers at Coseley Liberal Club, is a married woman and looks very emancipated for the period; she is seen here with her husband Harry on their motor-cycles.

Right: The May Queen, and her attendants, on their 'float', are thought to be from Roberts Street School, Lower Gornal in the early 1930s. Connie Beach (née Yates) is the May Queen.

Left: John Twigg Homer CBE, Deputy Lieutenant and County Alderman of Dormston House (see page 36).

Right: Mr and Mrs Church. Mrs F. Church had a millinery shop at 2 and 3 High Holborn. They were both prominent Primitive Methodists at the turn of the century.

A Hurst Hill couple, Mr and Mrs E. Waterhouse. Waterhouse's Screw Manufacturer's son married Miss Etheridge of the Coal Company (see Book 1).

The Sedgley Village Brass and Reed Band, probably *c.* 1920.

The most significant transport development in the Manor this century was the opening of the Birmingham New Road in November 1927. In May 1928 Coseley Council decided to line its length in the Urban District with memorial tree plantings to First World War victims. This photograph shows the Dedication and the crowds that gathered on the New Road, with Vicarage Road in the background.

Another scene of May 1928. The veterans gather to survey the trees.

The Birmingham New Road at Coseley in 1928 is striking for its emptiness and the fragility of the trees that were to grow to their maturity, with very little loss from vandalism! Each tree later received a small circle of railings, with a cast oval plate attached, bearing the name of each of the fallen.

In 1935 the damaged land that stood on the opposite side of the New Road to Vicarage Road became the Silver Jubilee Park. This is the opening ceremony. Councillor Jack Grange wears the chain of office and behind him, to the right, is J.C. Roper, Clerk to the Council.

The Second World War brought preparation for Civil Defence. With great ceremony a mobile canteen is 'launched'. It was to bring refreshment to the bombed out and the rescue services.

Prepared for a gas attack: the anti-gas squad on parade. Two figures most widely remembered are Dr Waddell (in the light suit) and Percy Bennett (next right). Mr Bennett was known as a Councillor and became Chairman of the Coseley Council, but he will also be remembered by older folk as the cheerful bus inspector with the Midland Red Bus Company, travelling along the New Road.

Making early use of the ornamental gates of the Silver Jubilee Park are helmeted Coseley firemen, posing in front of them with Councillor Stan Grange.

In wartime additional volunteer firemen were recruited, and all the local fire services were united as the National Fire Service.

Sedgley Home Guard relax at camp and manoeuvres at Bridgnorth. A bell tent has been erected at the rear.

Children enjoy winter sports in a field in Gospel End, off Dig Lane, towards Wood Farm, late 1960s. The reason for the slopes, so useful for tobogganing, is revealed by referring to the field name, Gravel Pit Piece, and in this case to a sixteenth-century activity.

In Baggeridge Woods.

This postcard of Baggeridge Wood, Gospel End, reveals a sister's pride in her brother's photographic skills, and also the general affection for this accessible section of the Earl of Dudley's estate. Local residents used it particularly well at the turn of the century, when long-distance travel was not generally within reach of the ordinary family.

In 1941, at the height of the war, this performance of Handel's *Messiah* by the Coseley United Choirs in the Clifton Cinema, Coseley, appears an act of defiance. To bring such numbers together in a public place, inviting an audience too, must have been seen as a bold move. The conductor was a well-known Coseley man, Jack Turley, and also of interest, on the extreme right in the middle row, is John S. Roper, solicitor and well-known local historian.

Coseley's Clifton Cinema was one of many in the Clifton chain, and stood facing the Memorial Gardens in Vicarage Road. This photograph was taken on the Sunday following its final Saturday performances, 11 August 1963.

The Cosy, Ivy House Lane, Coseley, was the earlier cinema, which was certainly in use from the 1920s. Sometimes it was known as Page's, after the local manager. It survived in the cinema boom years following the Second World War, but lost out in the great decline that hit all cinema chains.

Monday, May 19th. Full of suspense !
"TWO FOR DANGER" (A) featuring
Barry K. Barnes and Greta Gynt.
A thrilling jewel mystery that baffled
Scotland Yard !
Also—Edith Fellows in
"PRIDE OF THE BLUE GRASS" (U)

Thursday, May 22nd. Full of laughs !
**Priscilla Lane and Thomas Mitchell in
"THREE CHEERS for the IRISH"** (A)
You'll howl with delight at this grand
comedy drama of an Irish Policeman
—when he is forced into politics !

CHILDREN IN ARMS NOT ADMITTED

Our New Times :
MONDAY TO FRIDAY
Continuous from 6-30 to 10 p.m.
SATURDAYS ONLY
Continuous from 6-0 p.m. to 11 p.m.
Free Car Park for Patrons Only.
'Phone 2302.

Wm. Barrows (Printers) Ltd. Phone 3135

Western Electric
SOUND SYSTEM
Wide Range

What's On ?

DURING THE
MONTHS OF
APRIL—MAY
1941

Picture House

ADMISSION

7d.   10d.   1/2

Monday, April 21st.
A Grand Comedy Drama !
"DOWN WENT McGINTY" (A) with
**Brian Donlevy, Muriel Angelus and
Akim Tamiroff.**
Plenty of laughs and tense drama !
He'll fight any man and delight any
woman ! Also—"TALL TIMBERS" (U)

Thursday, April 24th. Magnificent !
Spencer Tracy in
"EDISON THE MAN" (U)
A great tribute . . great actor . . great
entertainment ! Spencer Tracy's
Greatest Performance !

Monday, April 28th. You'll enjoy.
"GOOD OLD SCHOOL DAYS" (U) with
William Holden and Bonita Granville.
A rousing, rollicking comedy, full of
mischief. Also—Jackie Cooper in
"LIFE WITH HENRY" (U)

Thursday, May 1st .Hectic adventure
Walter Pidgeon and Donald Meek
in **"PHANTOM RAIDERS"** (A)
A baffling and swiftly moving mystery
with suspense, excitement and entertainment in every foot

Monday, May 5th. It's a rib tickler !
William Powell and Myrna Loy
in **"I LOVE YOU AGAIN"** (A) with
Frank McHugh and Edmund Lowe.
Two grand stars in a grander comedy
—you'll enjoy every minute.

Thursday, May 8th. A reign of terror !
"QUEEN OF THE MOB" (A) featuring
Ralph Bellamy and Blanche Yurka.
Mother of a Devil's brood . . the most
vicious criminal brain of the under-
world ! Also—Charlie Ruggles in
"OPENED BY MISTAKE" (A)

Monday, May 12th. It's amusing !
Margaret Lockwood & Barry K. Barnes
in **"THE GIRL IN THE NEWS"** (A)
with **Emlyn Williams.** A gripping . . .
murder drama . . . tense and thrilling
. . . with a grand kick at the end !

Thursday, May 15th. A roaring tale !
"VIRGINIA CITY" (U) with
Errol Flynn and Miriam Hopkins.
Never so thrilling an adventure in so
mighty a picture. The screen thrill of
the year. 2 hours of enjoyment !

The smaller cinemas operated a twice-weekly change of film on Mondays and Thursdays; there were no
Sunday showings. This programme for April and May 1941 is actually from Jack Darby's, Upper Gornal
(featured in Book 1), but is typical of what might have been shown at the Cosy, or any of the smaller
district cinemas, of which there were many.

In earlier days, before National Insurance, or personal insurance plans, many people relied upon the good work of Death and Dividend clubs. Local branches of organizations like the Buffalos or the Foresters also provided aid. There were many guilds and lodges. This scroll of honour was awarded to an Upper Gornal man, Henry Beale, for the successful expansion of the National United Order of Free Gardeners at Dudley Lodge in 1911. Henry Beale may have been a gardener by hobby, but was employed at the Earl of Dudley's Round Oak Steelworks, Brierley Hill!

Coseley Council House, 1967. Lower Sedgley finally became Coseley Urban District, and with some pride they built their own Council House in 1895. The stone had been laid by Richard Clayton Esq JP, Chairman of the Council in that historic year.

Hurst Hill Rovers, 1908/9. Association Football was well established, and much local rivalry would have been expressed through the matches. From the photograph Hurst Hill Rovers were champions in this year. They pose proudly with their trophy, though the black armbands would suggest a mark of respect for someone deceased. The picture is taken in the yard of the Queen's Arms Inn, Hollywell Street (local sponsors?), and Carmi Bryan, the landlord, is the gentleman second from left on the top row.

One of Upper Gornal's annual events. Sam Jeavons dresses up his horse for May Day, photographed in 1936/7. On this occasion a touch of the circus has been introduced with the dog rider specially posed for the camera. His annual effort was recorded in the newspapers for many years after the Second World War.

Preparations in Upper Gornal for the Sedgley, Lower and Upper Gornal Carnival, around 1931, in the yard at Rock Street, Upper Gornal. The proceeds would probably have been for the Royal Hospital, Wolverhampton, for Mr W.G. Yates, a local funeral director, was a member of the committee. Brenda Burrows (née Hyde) is on the extreme left. Mrs Yates is cleaning her husband's bull-nosed Morris Cowley. Dressed for the carnival are, at the rear, Annie Cartwright (née Beale) and Bessie Nock (née Henderson) and, at the front, Connie Beach (née Yates) and Joyce Beale.

The Marsh family, who lived in Woodthorne, Lower Gornal (see page 44) are pictured here with their relations. Mr E. Marsh was a nearby local industrialist.

Sedgley Police Ball in the late 1960s. Included in the picture are Sgt Baxter, Dan Holden, Sgt Ken Lyon, ? Entwhistle, Cyril Hicken, Inspector Barsted, Arthur Golding, Mrs Entwhistle, Mrs Lyon, Brenda Baker and Mrs Barsted.

Well-known local personality, the late F. Andrew Barnett, headmaster of Redhall School, Lower Gornal, and local historian of the Manor. Joint founder of the Sedgley Local History Society, he was also an instigator of the plans for a Sedgley Museum. Here Andrew is doing what he enjoyed best, examining the hardened limestone core that suggests that limestone burning has taken place here in the Gorge, Hurst Hill.

Taking the air in Sedgley, *c.* 1920: a popular activity on the western slopes with walks across Kinsell and the Seven Cornfields most popular. The neat dress of this group might suggest an after church walk.

Wodehouse Road, Gospel End, as it approaches the houses and the Firs. The trees to the right are of Gospel End Common. This John Price postcard, from early this century, captures a lack of traffic long forgotten.

Brook Cottage, Penn Common.

John Price also recorded Brook Cottage and Penn Brook. Brook Cottage faces Nash's Coppice on the other side of the brook. As the brook provides the Manor boundary, the cow stands in Penn and looks into Gospel End.

BAGGERIDGE WOODS

Another view of Baggeridge Woods, Gospel End, shows the splendour of its walks with carefully fenced paths. Of all the villages Gospel End must have developed a miniature tourist trade, sustaining and refreshing the visitors from other parts of the Manor, and beyond, who visited Baggeridge and Penn Common. It was also not unknown for people to take a week's holiday there.

The Sugar Well, below Ellowes Hall and just in Lower Gornal, 1974. The limestone of the ridge provided many springs that over the years proved to be a blessing for local folks. This one would have been extensively used by the inhabitants of Ruiton in Upper Gornal, before an effective water supply was available – quite late in this century in some parts of the Manor.

The start of the Kinsell walk from Duck Lane, Sedgley (now Ettymore Road). It has all the characteristics of an ancient hollow way.

A surprising cast-iron post on the southern side footpath in Salop Street, Bradley (Brierley). To the east is B for Bilston Township, but to the west, as seen, is the S is for Sedgley.

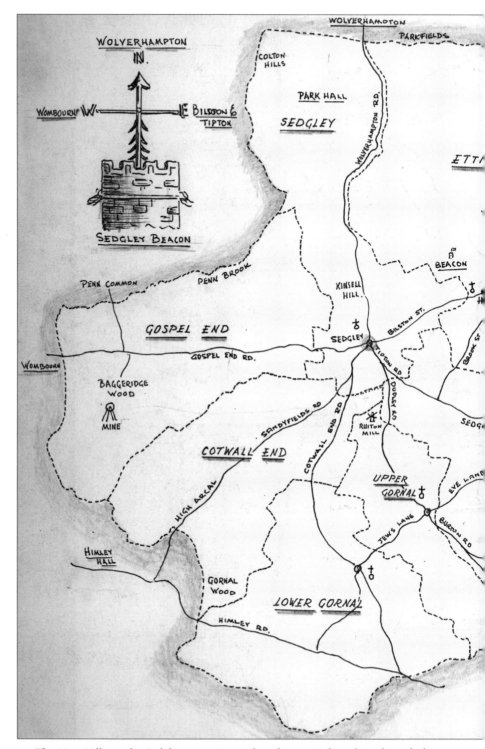

Sedgley Manor — The Nine Villages, by Sedgley artist Ron Baker, former Tailor of Quality Clothes, Sedgley High Street, and born in Woodsetton. F. Andrew Barnett meticulously plotted the village boundaries at the Tithe Survey of 1844. Using his research Ron Baker produced this map in 1996. Not all

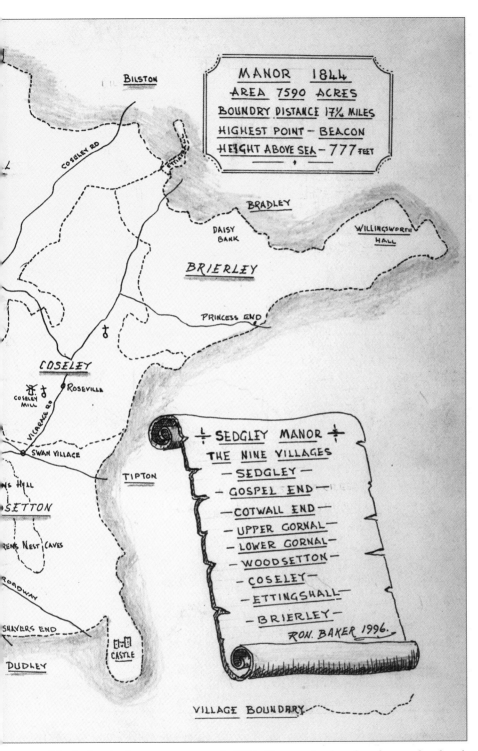

MANOR 1844
AREA 7590 ACRES
BOUNDRY DISTANCE 17¼ MILES
HIGHEST POINT — BEACON
HEIGHT ABOVE SEA — 777 FEET

SEDGLEY MANOR
THE NINE VILLAGES
— SEDGLEY —
— GOSPEL END —
— COTWALL END —
— UPPER GORNAL —
— LOWER GORNAL —
— WOODSETTON —
— COSELEY —
— ETTINGSHALL —
— BRIERLEY —
RON. BAKER 1996.

VILLAGE BOUNDARY

of the landmarks shown were present in 1844. The occasional road, and some churches shown, were not built at that time. They are included to aid the modern student in the task of locating in which ancient village they are standing within the Manor of Sedgley.

ACKNOWLEDGEMENTS

The author acknowledges his gratitude to the following:

Eddie Attwood, Brenda Baker, Denis Baker, Leslie Bates, Connie Beach, Joyce Beale, Howard Briscoe, Alan Carter, Bob Chesworth, Mary Clarke, Arthur and Sylvia Clements, Ra Cooper, George Cox, Ron Davies, the late J.T. Egginton, Marjorie Ellis, Cyril Field, Walter Goldie, John Grainger, David Haden, David Harrison, Fred and Betty Hill, Frank and Kitty Jones, Andrew Martin, Jean Powell, Neville Price, Freda Reynolds, Tom Roberts, Ken Slater, Chris Speake, Gladys Thomas, Dudley Metropolitan Borough Archives and Local History Service, Wolverhampton Metropolitan Borough Archives and Local Studies Centre, the Black Country Society, Mr Bryan Hollies and the Sedgley Museum.

Particular thanks to Mrs P. Margaret Roper for her own photographs, and also those of her late husband, John Roper. To Mrs Dews for, access to the photographs of her late husband, Richard Dews. To Mr Ron Baker for his own contributions and the help given in the search for material, and to the staff of COLAB Wolverhampton for their interest, advice and service.

Every effort has been made to contact all copyright holders of photographs where copyright has not originated with the person owning them.

THE BLACK COUNTRY SOCIETY

This voluntary society, affiliated to the Civic Trust, was founded in 1967 as a reaction to the trend of the late 1950s and early 1960s to amalgamate everything into large units and in the Midlands to sweep away the area's industrial heritage in the process.

The general aim of the Society is to create interest in the past, present and future of the Black Country, and early on it campaigned for the establishment of an industrial museum. In 1975 the Black Country Museum was started by Dudley Borough Council on 26 acres of totally derelict land adjoining the grounds of Dudley Castle. This has developed into an award-winning museum which attracts over 250,000 visitors annually.

At the Black Country Museum there is a boat dock fully equipped to restore narrow boats of wood and iron and different boats can be seen on the dock throughout the year. From behind the Bottle and Glass Inn visitors can travel on a canal boat into Dudley Canal Tunnel, a memorable journey to see spectacular limestone caverns and the fascinating Castle Mill Basin.

There are over two thousand members of the Black Country Society and all receive the quarterly magazine *The Blackcountryman*, of which over 119 issues have been published since its founding in 1967. In the whole collection there are some 1,700 authoritative articles on all aspects of the Black Country by historians, teachers, researchers, students, subject experts and ordinary folk with an extraordinary story to tell. The whole constitutes a unique resource about the area and is a mine of information for students and researchers who frequently refer to it. Many schools and libraries are subscribers. Three thousand copies of the magazine are printed each quarter. It is non-commercial, and contributors do not receive payment for their articles.

PO Box 71 · Kingswinford · West Midlands DY6 9YN

BRITAIN IN OLD PHOTOGRAPHS

Aberystwyth & North Ceredigion
Around Abingdon
Acton
Alderney: A Second Selection
Along the Avon from Stratford to
  Tewkesbury
Altrincham
Amersham
Around Amesbury
Anglesey
Arnold & Bestwood
Arnold & Bestwood: A Second
  Selection
Arundel & the Arun Valley
Ashbourne
Around Ashby-de-la-Zouch
Avro Aircraft
Aylesbury
Balham & Tooting
Banburyshire
Barnes, Mortlake & Sheen
Barnsley
Bath
Beaconsfield
Bedford
Bedfordshire at Work
Bedworth
Beverley
Bexley
Bideford
Bilston
Birmingham Railways
Bishop's Stortford &
  Sawbridgeworth
Bishopstone & Seaford
Bishopstone & Seaford: A Second
  Selection
Black Country Aviation
Black Country Railways
Black Country Road Transport
Blackburn
Blackpool
Around Blandford Forum
Bletchley
Bolton
Bournemouth
Bradford
Braintree & Bocking at Work
Brecon
Brentwood
Bridgwater & the River Parrett
Bridlington
Bridport & the Bride Valley
Brierley Hill
Brighton & Hove
Brighton & Hove: A Second
  Selection
Bristol
Around Bristol
Brixton & Norwood
Early Broadstairs & St Peters
Bromley, Keston & Hayes

Buckingham & District
Burford
Bury
Bushbury
Camberwell
Cambridge
Cannock Yesterday & Today
Canterbury: A Second Selection
Castle Combe to Malmesbury
Chadwell Heath
Chard & Ilminster
Chatham Dockyard
Chatham & Gillingham
Cheadle
Cheam & Belmont
Chelmsford
Cheltenham: A Second Selection
Cheltenham at War
Cheltenham in the 1950s
Chepstow & the River Wye
Chesham Yesterday & Today
Cheshire Railways
Chester
Chippenham & Lacock
Chiswick
Chorley & District
Cirencester
Around Cirencester
Clacton-on-Sea
Around Clitheroe
Clwyd Railways
Clydesdale
Colchester
Colchester 1940–70
Colyton & Seaton
The Cornish Coast
Corsham & Box
The North Cotswolds
Coventry: A Second Selection
Around Coventry
Cowes & East Cowes
Crawley New Town
Around Crawley
Crewkerne & the Ham Stone
  Villages
Cromer
Croydon
Crystal Palace, Penge & Anerley
Darlington
Darlington: A Second Selection
Dawlish & Teignmouth
Deal
Derby
Around Devizes
Devon Aerodromes
East Devon at War
Around Didcot & the Hagbournes
Dorchester
Douglas
Dumfries
Dundee at Work
Durham People

Durham at Work
Ealing & Northfields
East Grinstead
East Ham
Eastbourne
Elgin
Eltham
Ely
Enfield
Around Epsom
Esher
Evesham to Bredon
Exeter
Exmouth & Budleigh Salterton
Fairey Aircraft
Falmouth
Farnborough
Farnham: A Second Selection
Fleetwood
Folkestone: A Second Selection
Folkestone: A Third Selection
The Forest of Dean
Frome
Fulham
Galashiels
Garsington
Around Garstang
Around Gillingham
Gloucester
Gloucester: from the Walwin
  Collection
North Gloucestershire at War
South Gloucestershire at War
Gosport
Goudhurst to Tenterden
Grantham
Gravesend
Around Gravesham
Around Grays
Great Yarmouth
Great Yarmouth: A Second
  Selection
Greenwich & Woolwich
Grimsby
Around Grimsby
Grimsby Docks
Gwynedd Railways
Hackney: A Second Selection
Hackney: A Third Selection
From Haldon to Mid-Dartmoor
Hammersmith & Shepherds Bush
Hampstead to Primrose Hill
Harrow & Pinner
Hastings
Hastings: A Second Selection
Haverfordwest
Hayes & West Drayton
Around Haywards Heath
Around Heathfield
Around Heathfield: A Second
  Selection
Around Helston

Around Henley-on-Thames
Herefordshire
Herne Bay
Heywood
The High Weald
The High Weald: A Second
  Selection
Around Highworth
Around Highworth & Faringdon
Hitchin
Holderness
Honiton & the Otter Valley
Horsham & District
Houghton-le-Spring &
  Hetton-le-Hole
Houghton-le-Spring & Hetton-le-
  Hole: A Second Selection
Huddersfield: A Second Selection
Huddersfield: A Third Selection
Ilford
Ilfracombe
Ipswich: A Second Selection
Islington
Jersey: A Third Selection
Kendal
Kensington & Chelsea
East Kent at War
Keswick & the Central Lakes
Around Keynsham & Saltford
The Changing Face of Keynsham
Kingsbridge
Kingston
Kinver
Kirkby & District
Kirkby Lonsdale
Around Kirkham
Knowle & Dorridge
The Lake Counties at Work
Lancashire
The Lancashire Coast
Lancashire North of the Sands
Lancashire Railways
East Lancashire at War
Around Lancaster
Lancing & Sompting
Around Leamington Spa
Around Leamington Spa:
  A Second Selection
Leeds in the News
Leeds Road & Rail
Around Leek
Leicester
The Changing Face of Leicester
Leicester at Work
Leicestershire People
Around Leighton Buzzard &
  Linslade
Letchworth
Lewes
Lewisham & Deptford:
  A Second Selection
Lichfield

Lincoln
Lincoln Cathedral
The Lincolnshire Coast
Liverpool
Around Llandudno
Around Lochaber
Theatrical London
Around Louth
The Lower Fal Estuary
Lowestoft
Luton
Lympne Airfield
Lytham St Annes
Maidenhead
Around Maidenhead
Around Malvern
Manchester
Manchester Road & Rail
Mansfield
Marlborough: A Second Selection
Marylebone & Paddington
Around Matlock
Melton Mowbray
Around Melksham
The Mendips
Merton & Morden
Middlesbrough
Midsomer Norton & Radstock
Around Mildenhall
Milton Keynes
Minehead
Monmouth & the River Wye
The Nadder Valley
Newark
Around Newark
Newbury
Newport, Isle of Wight
The Norfolk Broads
Norfolk at War
North Fylde
North Lambeth
North Walsham & District
Northallerton
Northampton
Around Norwich
Nottingham 1944–74
The Changing Face of Nottingham
Victorian Nottingham
Nottingham Yesterday & Today
Nuneaton
Around Oakham
Ormskirk & District
Otley & District
Oxford: The University
Oxford Yesterday & Today
Oxfordshire Railways: A Second Selection
Oxfordshire at School
Around Padstow
Pattingham & Wombourne

Penwith
Penzance & Newlyn
Around Pershore
Around Plymouth
Poole
Portsmouth
Poulton-le-Fylde
Preston
Prestwich
Pudsey
Radcliffe
RAF Chivenor
RAF Cosford
RAF Hawkinge
RAF Manston
RAF Manston: A Second Selection
RAF St Mawgan
RAF Tangmere
Ramsgate & Thanet Life
Reading
Reading: A Second Selection
Redditch & the Needle District
Redditch: A Second Selection
Richmond, Surrey
Rickmansworth
Around Ripley
The River Soar
Romney Marsh
Romney Marsh: A Second Selection
Rossendale
Around Rotherham
Rugby
Around Rugeley
Ruislip
Around Ryde
St Albans
St Andrews
Salford
Salisbury
Salisbury: A Second Selection
Salisbury: A Third Selection
Around Salisbury
Sandhurst & Crowthorne
Sandown & Shanklin
Sandwich
Scarborough
Scunthorpe
Seaton, Lyme Regis & Axminster
Around Seaton & Sidmouth
Sedgley & District
The Severn Vale
Sherwood Forest
Shrewsbury
Shrewsbury: A Second Selection
Shropshire Railways
Skegness
Around Skegness
Skipton & the Dales
Around Slough

Smethwick
Somerton & Langport
Southampton
Southend-on-Sea
Southport
Southwark
Southwell
Southwold to Aldeburgh
Stafford
Around Stafford
Staffordshire Railways
Around Staveley
Stepney
Stevenage
The History of Stilton Cheese
Stoke-on-Trent
Stoke Newington
Stonehouse to Painswick
Around Stony Stratford
Around Stony Stratford: A Second Selection
Stowmarket
Streatham
Stroud & the Five Valleys
Stroud & the Five Valleys: A Second Selection
Stroud's Golden Valley
The Stroudwater and Thames & Severn Canals
The Stroudwater and Thames & Severn Canals: A Second Selection
Suffolk at Work
Suffolk at Work: A Second Selection
The Heart of Suffolk
Sunderland
Sutton
Swansea
Swindon: A Third Selection
Swindon: A Fifth Selection
Around Tamworth
Taunton
Around Taunton
Teesdale
Teesdale: A Second Selection
Tenbury Wells
Around Tettenhall & Codshall
Tewkesbury & the Vale of Gloucester
Thame to Watlington
Around Thatcham
Around Thirsk
Thornbury to Berkeley
Tipton
Around Tonbridge
Trowbridge
Around Truro
TT Races
Tunbridge Wells

Tunbridge Wells: A Second Selection
Twickenham
Uley, Dursley & Cam
The Upper Fal
The Upper Tywi Valley
Uxbridge, Hillingdon & Cowley
The Vale of Belvoir
The Vale of Conway
Ventnor
Wakefield
Wallingford
Walsall
Waltham Abbey
Wandsworth at War
Wantage, Faringdon & the Vale Villages
Around Warwick
Weardale
Weardale: A Second Selection
Wednesbury
Wells
Welshpool
West Bromwich
West Wight
Weston-super-Mare
Around Weston-super-Mare
Weymouth & Portland
Around Wheatley
Around Whetstone
Whitchurch to Market Drayton
Around Whitstable
Wigton & the Solway Plain
Willesden
Around Wilton
Wimbledon
Around Windsor
Wingham, Addisham & Littlebourne
Wisbech
Witham & District
Witney
Around Witney
The Witney District
Wokingham
Around Woodbridge
Around Woodstock
Woolwich
Woolwich Royal Arsenal
Around Wootton Bassett, Cricklade & Purton
Worcester
Worcester in a Day
Around Worcester
Worcestershire at Work
Around Worthing
Wotton-under-Edge to Chipping Sodbury
Wymondham & Attleborough
The Yorkshire Wolds

To order any of these titles please telephone our distributor, Littlehampton Book Services on 01903 721596
For a catalogue of these and our other titles please ring Regina Schinner on 01453 731114